SUCCESSFUL USE OF NEW
MATHEMATICAL MODELS

Successful Use
of New
Mathematical Models

Dr. Sam R. Goodman

Prentice-Hall's Financial Management Series

Prentice-Hall, Inc.   *Englewood Cliffs, N.J.*

PRINTED IN THE UNITED STATES OF AMERICA
ISBN-0-13-875401-2
ENCY

MLW

TABLE OF CONTENTS

THE ESSENCE OF FINANCIAL MODELS

Total information is not a virtue. In fact, it can be an eroding vice (vise?). In fact, so many misconceptions have arisen around the theme of mathematical models for financial planning that many companies have now seen fit to disband this area of computer applications and have reverted back to utilizing the two basic resources of the efficient executive—his brain and his hand. In fact, during the economic downturn which took place in 1970, many corporate and computer operations research executives for the first time had something in common with their advertising and research and development counterparts; they were the first to have their jobs cut out from under them during times of employment retrenchment. Even a man such as David Hertz, a computer expert, has said, "It hasn't been clearly demonstrated yet that computers are helpful to the top management process."

Some years ago, Merle Crawford wrote an article called "The Shotgun Marriage Between Mathematics and Marketing" in which he expressed the opinion that exotic marketing models were largely a failure because of the inability of the model-oriented man to communicate to the individual who is not necessarily so oriented. He complained that in many respects the technically-oriented people had developed a jargon of their own and, in fact, had built a castle with a moat around it into which only those who are privy to the jargon could enter. In a large sense, the jargon problem has a great deal to do with the effectiveness of corporate model-building for financial planning. At the outset, let me state my opinion that I do believe that there are effective corporate models for financial planning, but they are pitifully few. I also believe that it is an evolutionary way of the future which will become more effective and more widespread as the limitations of such models are more widely understood. The challenge, after all, in a simulation program which is the essence of a model, is to capture the essence of a total organization. Even before the model is created, it is created with an impossible objective. No one can ever be sure that any plan has accounted for all of the alternatives among the choices which can be made, nor can we be sure that all of the relevant inputs have been included. This, though, need not be a constraining criterion for limiting the effective use of corporate models. An analogy might be drawn to the automobile which may be driven despite the fact that the carburetor may not be in the best shape nor the brake linings completely perfect. The essence of the argument is that the automobile nevertheless does take you from one destination to the other.

A Simulation Program

A simulation program, the essence of the model, is in reality a mixture of determinable facts, certain assumptions regarding the future, judgments as to the sensitivities of variables, calculations which are intrinsic to the business, and, above all, human intuition—guesses, if you will. And largely, this combination of characteristics takes the physical form of an iceberg because the model in the final analysis is reduced to a workable combination of mathematical formulae. The formulae, however, take on the profile of a piece of matter. Because in order to construct the visible portion of the model which is the end product, the input data which is used for the model has undergone a series of massages which have taken on the appearance of atoms, nuclei and subparticles of matter. In other words, it is a process of reducing complex systems which in turn have subsystems, which in turn have subsystems feeding them. The model, therefore, is an extremely complex piece of achievement which is constantly changing and constantly growing. Any model in order to be effective must be a flexible model and capable of producing its output in a manner which is understandable to the user and, moreover, it must be a model which is oriented toward pragmatic decision-making.

THE PEOPLE INVOLVED IN THE MODEL PROCESS

The computer has already had a major effect on the financial profession as it serves private companies. In using the term "financial profession," I am alluding to the accounting staffs for the most part, along with financial planning personnel if they are separate. Regretfully, however, many in the financial profession, including practicing public accountants, view the application of financial planning more in terms of budgeting than they do in true simulation.

There is a distinct difference between a plan and a budget and unfortunately the public accounting restrictive view of budgeting hinders true financial planning whether through the application of model-building or not. A financial plan is a true guide, a road map. The plan has an objective, the road map shows the various routes, the side streets, the crossroads, the alternative choices as to how to reach the destination. It is easy to trace that road which can bring the driver most easily to his destination in the shortest and safest time.

The budget on the other hand, is very much like a two-lane highway. There is a right side to the road and a left side to the road and the driver must stay somewhere in between the right side and the left side if he is to stay within the budget. The end objective, of course, may still be the same.

However, in terms of practicing business problems, I have too often seen situations where close to the end of the year individuals have discovered that they have not made expenditures in the amount of the budget and therefore they have turned around and said, "By golly, I've still got $300 thousand to spend and I'll find a way to spend it before the end of the year." Planning models do not deal with this latter type of situation. They are much more concerned with the former. This type of orientation, which stems from the rigidity of financial disciplines which are inherent in the training of most financial individuals, leads me to suspect that the burden of construction for financial planning models will ultimately, if it has not already done so, fall into the specialized area of operations research.

John Dearden, in an article, once indicated that one of the difficulties facing practicing operations research personnel is that unlike other professionals, such as lawyers, doctors or accountants, the cross which the operations researchers had to bear is that they continuously have to explain what their discipline is. That by itself creates terrible difficulties in trying to reach the practical, pragmatic business executive.

Operations Research

Operations research is a wide area of activity. It certainly is not a new or mysterious profession which has sprung up in response to the fact that a computer exists. This is not a question of Parkinson's Law as it applies to the creation of new professions. In fact, operations research involves an extension of many of the techniques, ideas and principles which have been used by business for many years. What has happened, though, is that all of this body has been compressed into a formal and recognized discipline which now has a proper name. In its essence, though, it is an attitude. The American Management Association in one of its papers, says that the operations research approach to a business problem involves the following basic steps:

1. Observation and general study of the problem area
2. Definition of the problem
3. Fact-finding
4. Analysis of the data and construction of a model or hypothesis
5. Comparison of the model with observed data
6. Repetition of each step, if the model proves not in agreement with observed data, until a satisfactory model is constructed

Dearden adds in one of his papers that a descriptive type of definition is also needed to assist the understanding of the technical definition. He cites the following elements of operations research as being characteristics of the operation:

a. There is a team approach to problem solving
b. The members of the team represent different areas of expertise of scientific background
c. There is a mathematical model
d. There is interaction and involvement with the decision makers

Each of the foregoing citations begins to lower the level of the water around the iceberg by fractions of an inch so that underneath the top we are now beginning to expose the layer of complexity involved in model-building. At this juncture, though, it is probably appropriate to add that these caveats which are being offered regarding the complexities of model-building are not intended to frighten off the reader from either considering or utilizing these techniques. Many facilities are available which are relatively inexpensive to use and which still incorporate the essence of model-building.

It is still a truism that there are not many companies doing very extensive operations research work. However, there are a number of companies which are finding interesting uses for variants of operations research techniques. William Vatter in his most interesting study, published in *The Accounting Review* demonstrated very clearly that the search for effective uses of mathematical models continues, however, in areas which are alien to simulation and model-building. Companies interviewed in his questionnaire overwhelmingly applied the greater part of their operations research techniques to studies involving factor analysis, queuing models, linear programming models and various regression analyses.

Dearden indicates that he feels that there are four general categories of tools for formal operations research methods. He cites these as, financial models, statistical models, mathematical programming and simulations. He is correct in observing that financial models have been with us for some time. He observes that, in fact, business would be lost without them. He makes the important observation, though, that because simulation techniques did not appear until the decade of the sixties, it is clear why operations research has become so closely identified with mathematical programming, especially linear programming. Of course, the operations research which we are discussing in the context of this paper goes far beyond linear programming techniques and, indeed, we will progress in short order to the financial model in particular.

It is probable that if planning models are to become effective, changes in basic corporate organization will also have to be created. One of the reasons for the essential failure of operations research as a functioning management group has been the fact that operations research personnel, for the most part, do not have access to the highest levels of management where decisions are made. As a result, they have frequently been derided and their profession misunderstood. Nevertheless, it should not detract from the value of the operation.

It would appear to me that the soundest approach to an effective organizational concept for decision-making is to establish a separate functioning area for management sciences. This separate area should be independent of the data processing system. For too long management science techniques have been associated with the computer and more often, operations research and systems groups have found themselves reporting to the head of data processing. In essence, this is an anomaly because the two fields can be very alien to each other. Just as physical distribution should be an independent reporting function, so should operations research.

Artists and Models

One of the first things that is necessary to accomplish in order to continue the discussion of model-building and proceed toward its application in financial planning is to define the precise nature of a model. A model purports to be a representation of the real world. It is a computer program which has as its basis input mathematical equations. These in turn are designed to simulate realistic business situations and reflect the operating nature of the business.

Generally the model is completely mathematical. The challenge in the creation of models is to build one which will react and produce results which are likely to mirror actual operations. Clark Sloat indicates that he felt it was possible to identify different relationships with well-known scientific theories and as a result, include the data in a form which has been proven by scientific experiments. He says that the use of mathematical expressions is scientifically determinable and can be relied upon for probabilities and further that product demands can be identified with known types of distribution curves, so that he felt that, over a period of time, there was a correlation of actual results with predictive results.

George Gershefski wrote a fine paper for the Planning Executives Institute recently dealing with the development and applications of a corporate financial model. In the course of writing that paper, he cited some of the work done for the Sun Oil Company. One of the more valuable aspects of that paper was a question and answer session which he used as a base for expanding on the concept of the Sun model. Because of the relevance of his observations to the subject being discussed, it is appropriate here to review some of Mr. Gershefski's feelings about different aspects of model building, especially as it concerns financial planning:

. . . Once developed, a model provides accurate projections rapidly and inexpensively; it is comprehensive and follows a precise documented procedure. In short, management can be quickly provided with meaningful decision-oriented information.

. . . Models are extremely valuable for comparing and evaluating alternative courses of action that might be followed; by compiling the results of feasible alternative plans, they can provide management with information which is helpful in determining realistic objectives for the corporation. Models are also useful in short-term profit planning by providing an independent estimate of net income for gauging how well current operations meet management targets for profitability, growth and stability. Finally, models are an efficient means for developing a revised estimate of income when originally planned circumstances are expected to change. It is important to note that models neither create plans nor make decisions; they do, however, provide structured information to aid in these processes. Models will be most effective when employed in a company which plans on a formal basis and which follows a style of management by objectives.

. . . A chess game can provide another view of the concept of a model. If, in addition to the board on which the game is being played, one of the players has another chessboard set up beside him with the pieces in identical positions as in the real game he could move the pieces to determine the outcome of various strategies in advance of his actual move. The chess set at his side would serve as a model of the real game.

Examples of Functional Model Applications

At this point, it should be somewhat obvious to the reader that a model can be many things and that there are various applications within corporate life for models. The applications extend into various fields. Some of the better known examples of functional model applications are for:

- warehousing and distribution
- inventory control
- sales forecasting
- production scheduling
- large volume of processing
- distribution costs
- decision simulations
- labor negotiation models
- capital budgeting

- product pricing
- portfolio analysis
- risk analysis for product innovations

No function within a business or no element of the business is an island unto itself. If I were to paraphrase John Donne, each function is, "A piece of the continent; a part of the main." For example, Exhibit 1 shows the conceptual view of a new product model which is currently in use by Detroit Diesel Allyson, which is a division of General Motors in Indiana. Looking at the concept of the new product model, it is obvious to the viewer that many elements of the "marketing" new product model involve relevant inputs which are related to financial planning. Even within this somewhat simplified view of the model, the following are various inputs required from financial planning:

Capital investment

Production expenses

Fixed manufacturing costs

All of the relevant accounting data involving:
   working capital
   depreciation
   unit prices, etc.

The output for the model is expressed in terms of return on investment with a stockholders' eyeview of the result. In addition, the following are decision outputs stemming from the model:

Annual cash flows

Annual profits before and after taxes

Annual dollar sales

Present value

Annual lost sales

Sensitivity analysis

This latter phrase, sensitivity analysis, is an interesting newcomer to the jargon of model-building. In reality, sensitivity analysis is nothing more than the consideration of possible changes in the basic data input for a given problem. The consideration of the changes measures the effect of such changes on the final result. It is also an examination of the magnitude of change required in basic data before the entrance of new data is applied to the final basic solution.

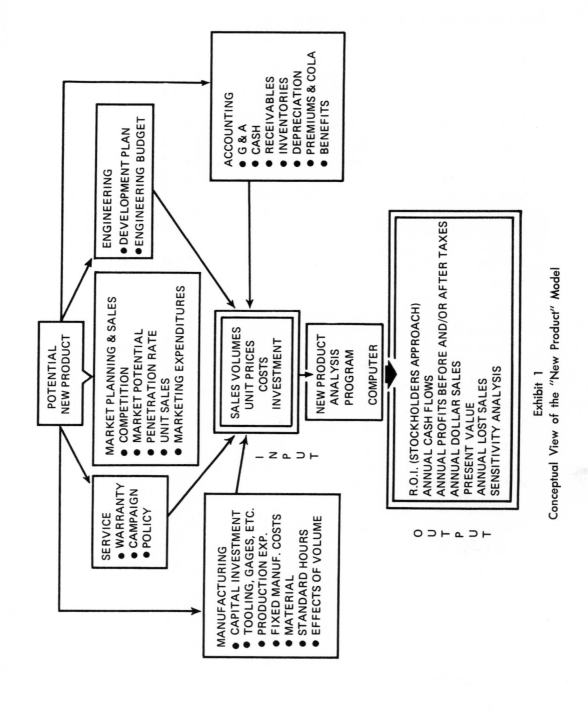

Exhibit 1
Conceptual View of the "New Product" Model

14

THE DESIGN OF THE MODEL

Michael Tyran wrote recently that, in order to develop an effective and appropriate projection model, certain common considerations are inherent in most design systems. He cites the following:

1. Data requirements
2. Manual procedures
3. Participating organizations
4. Level of sophistication
5. Level of process
6. Organization structure composition
7. Assessment of historical data
8. Specific flow and data interface

A predecessor even to these steps is the formulation of a corporate objective or goal to be integrated into the model. George Gershefski in his paper cites the following as the sequence to help management achieve that very first step:

> The first step in all planning is collecting pertinent information from each department of the company. Complete data on operations and costs are not required at this stage; only those forecasts or assumptions necessary to make a projection with the model are needed. Generally, this is less than that required to make a full-scale budget projection because of the equation and relationship within the model.
>
> There is also a change in emphasis. As an example, the investment and the sales volume for a typical marketing outlet are requested. The total sales volume is *not* to be estimated at this point since it depends on the total amount of capital allocated to the sales effort and the investment and volume per outlet. The capital allocation, in turn, depends on management's profitability and growth targets which are being determined as a result of this process.
>
> After having collected the required forecasts, the next step is to develop and to evaluate various planning alternatives. As an illustration, consider a company which has two areas competing for capital: the marketing segment and the raw material supply, or production, segment. To determine the consequences of investing in one area versus the other,

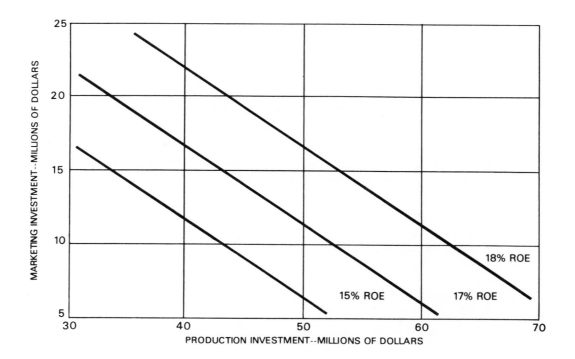

Illustration 1

the financial model projects profitability assuming different investment allocations between the two. The results of a number of allocations are summarized in Illustration 1. The chart shows the amount of money invested in production along the horizontal axis and the amount of money invested in marketing along the vertical axis. To construct the diagram, the return on equity for each case is plotted versus the amount of money allocated to each area. Points with the same return on equity are connected to form a line of equal value. Illustration 1 is based on hypothetical data and implies that cases of equal value formed a straight line. One line, for example, is labeled 18 percent return on stockholders' equity. This means that any combination of investment mix that falls on this line will earn 18 percent return on stockholders' equity. A production investment of $40 million along with a marketing investment of $22 million would result in an 18 percent return, as would a $60 million production investment along with a $12 million marketing investment.

When an approach of this type is taken, problems evolve outside of the model which must be analyzed and resolved. For example, in a particular case there may be inadequate manufacturing capacity to handle the market share considered. If so, it is necessary to determine the manufacturing facilities required, submit the appropriate changes to the model, and re-examine the investment allocations.

Once realistic forecasts have been made, executive management selects that investment allocation or combination of alternative plans which will meet the corporate goals as they define them. Return on equity is the management goal in this illustration. However, management may also be interested in such items as earnings per share, percent debt in the capital structure and earnings stability. Thus, they may choose an investment of $50 million in production and $16.5 million in marketing since it yields an 18 percent return and provides the most satisfactory level of achievement relative to other management aims.

A model projects the anticipated performance for each department of the company to determine the total corporate outlook. Thus, choosing a corporate target also implies an operating plan and investment level for each area. In the case of marketing, for example, the amount of money to be invested would be determined directly; this can be translated into a specific sales objective. If each department accomplished the designated tasks, then the company as a whole will attain the desired goals.

At this point in the process, detailed plans and budgets are prepared by each department to meet the desired objectives. A consolidation of the individual plans results in an overall profit plan for the coming period. This step is followed by the usual ones of comparing actual with planned results and of determining reasons for any variations. If the economic outlook changes substantially, it may be necessary to repeat the process since revised goals may be appropriate.

All models begin with the initial input of data. An example of the data flow for an organizational financial plan is shown in Exhibit 2. Based upon this type of organization for requiring data flow, models can be created for the various areas which were cited earlier.

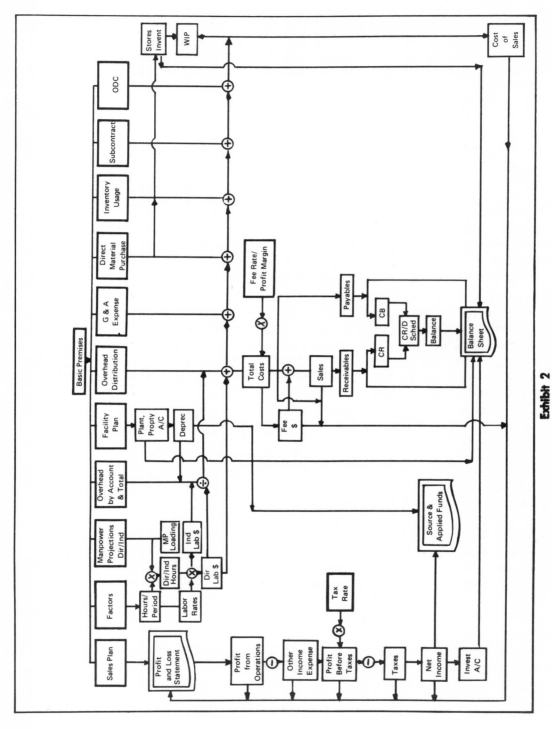

Exhibit 2

Organization Financial Plan—Data Flow

(Michael R. Tyran, "A Computerized Decision-Simulator Model," *Management Accounting*, March 1971, p. 21)

18

INVENTORY CONTROL MODELS

The Vatter study referred to earlier indicated that one of the most popular fields for the application of modeling techniques is in inventory control. Inventory control lends itself to modeling techniques because, generally speaking, the variables inherent in inventory levels are not nearly so susceptible to change as they are in, for instance, marketing problems.

Most practicing executives are familiar with the expression EOQ. The initials stand for the expression "Economic Order Quantity." This is a statistical procedure whereby inventories are theoretically optimized by automatic repurchase patterns. The essence of inventory management involves a problem of a delicate balance of costs. These costs necessarily are opportunity costs; they are the costs of alternative actions.

Certainly the penalty for carrying excess inventory involves severe charges and the inflation of working capital requirements. The risks that are inherent in a poor inventory policy include those of obsolescence and damage to materials. In addition, space costs, inventories, taxes, and imputed interests are real considerations in the level of inventory maintenance. The word "optimized" was used previously for a specific purpose.

There is absolutely no virtue in attempting to achieve an inventory policy which will assure that all distribution points have sufficient stock to make all orders to customers at the time that all orders are requested. Any system that will attempt to achieve 100 percent coverage of requirements is a costly system and can be proven statistically unprofitable. A far better minimization program involves that of balancing the costs of carrying the inventories sufficient for 100 percent deliveries against the cost of being out-of-stock. The cost for being out of stock is an opportunity cost which is inherent in the risk that a consumer may not come back to purchase an item if it is not found to be immediately available.

It is, of course, possible to live on a day-to-day basis and frequently have stock-outs. No company with any operating intelligence could afford this type of program since it would inevitably be detrimental to its commercial policy. The basic question then arises, as was stated by Clark Sloat, as to "How much inventory we should carry and when we should reorder the various items we are required to use so that we can maintain a reasonable balance between the costs of carrying inventories, the costs of running out-of-stock and the costs of purchasing materials."

It is a truism that the importance of inventory largely depends on the nature of the individual industry. Obviously, service industries do not suffer the same inventory penalties as do purely commercial industries.

The problem can be looked at really only in one way. William Parks wrote that only one goal is really appropriate for any inventory system. But in his view it can be expressed in either of two ways—to minimize the total cost or alternatively, to maximize the profit within a specified time, considering the various resource requirements. Further, when opportunity costs are included in the total cost, it is his view that the aims are identical. Total costs in this sense can be defined as a combination of *order costs*. This is a cost which is incurred when ordering merchandise or establishing the mechanics of making the material available.

Carrying Costs

Carrying costs are expenses which are generally associated with the cost of capital, insurance, storage costs, obsolescence, spoilage costs and the cost of not having the alternative investment opportunities because inventories are in stock.

Shortage Costs

Shortage costs were referred to earlier as the cost of being out-of-stock when the merchandise is requested by a customer. In this sense, this type of cost includes the actual penalty of being deprived of the profit margin and, in an opportunity sense, the cost of never regaining the customer.

Most statistical texts teach that the EOQ formula is the best inventory control system in the traditional sense. Mr. Parks indicates that in his view it is inadequate for practical commercial use for the following reasons:

1. The formula assumes that the costs of being out-of-stock are relatively insignificant and thus can be ignored for the most part. In this sense, it is his contention that it fails to recognize one of the three earlier cited main costs of carrying inventory.
2. It fails to allow for comparisons of low points on several curves simultaneously, thereby rendering itself useless when quantity discounts are available. In other words, the EOQ formula is adequate only when no quantity discounts for purchasing are involved in the sales policy of the company.
3. It fails to provide an estimation of variation, thereby necessitating an arbitrary safety stock, an item not provided for in computing the *best order quantity*.

Traditional Definitions

Traditional EOQ quantities are found by minimizing the total cost when that cost is defined as including only carrying costs and the basic order costs as well as the initial basic material costs. The following traditional definitions are given for inclusion in the formula for economic order quantities. They are, following Parks, as follows:

$$TC = \text{Total cost}$$
$$Q = \text{Order quantity}$$
$$O = \text{Order cost}$$
$$T = \text{Material cost}$$
$$C = \text{Carrying cost}$$
$$K = \text{Annual demand}$$

The derivation of the formula, although necessary, is not particularly significant to the discussion, therefore, based upon calculus, the final formula for EOQ is determined as follows:

$$EOQ = \sqrt{\frac{2KO}{CT}}$$

One of the difficulties in the EOQ equation is the cost of determining the penalty for being out-of-stock. Even if the answer cannot be explicitly calculated, an attempt should be made to make an approximate estimate for the cost of being out-of-stock based upon the probabilities of repurchase. This is necessary because the only realistic method of determining an inventory reorder point must consider the interplay between the factors of cost.

In other words, at the best level, carrying costs and shortage costs are equal. In that respect, it is somewhat analogous to the discounted cash flow calculation in which an interest rate is sought that will equalize both inflow and outgo. Parks points out that the reorder point should be increased until the carrying cost of adding one more unit to the inventory just balances the expected costs of being out-of-stock.

Certainly the techniques for inventory models are derived from statistically complex formulas, some involving the Poisson distribution, which is a method of describing a series of independent events. In some instances, management service areas of major accounting firms who have tackled the inventory control problem have been able to achieve a reduction of at least fifteen to twenty percent in inventory levels while still maintaining adequate customer service as defined by the respective managements of the companies. It is expected naturally that not every company can afford either the management services area of major accounting firms or their own operations research staffs. At the very least, however, the IMPACT program, which is a "canned" program for inventory control offered by IBM, is available for purchase and has proven to be a highly effective instrument for inventory control.

Warehouse	Market Requirements	Unit Transportation Costs From Plants				
		1	2	3	4	5
A	50 M	$.250	$.375	$.375	$.500	$.175
B	250	.175	.250	.325	.450	.140
C	75	.100	.225	.275	.425	.175
D	25	.140	.220	.225	.425	.190
E	30	.195	.190	.150	.400	.220
F	40	.325	.210	.175	.235	.315
G	50	.350	.190	.150	.210	.325
H	200	.290	.190	.220	.125	.240
I	60	.295	.175	.190	.110	.250
J	40	.220	.090	.210	.150	.215
K	20	.450	.200	.175	.175	.340
L	150	.175	.350	.275	.325	.175
M	70	.200	.350	.300	.325	.200
N	10	.225	.375	.325	.350	.225
	1,070 M					
Productive Capacity	1,300 M	250 M	300 M	250 M	300 M	200 M
Unit Production Cost		$4.00	$3.50	$2.50	$4.00	$3.50

Exhibit 3

MODEL USES IN PHYSICAL DISTRIBUTION

The problems inherent in the physical distribution function include some of the problems already cited in inventories. However, because of the diversity of the function and its place as an arbitrator between production capacity and sales requirements, the questions of physical distribution often find themselves placed in an allied but distinctly different pattern from those of inventory control. For example, practical business questions often arise which ask:

a. What is the optimum location for our warehouses?
b. Which manufacturing plant is best located to service the various warehouses?
c. What type of transportation should be utilized to deliver merchandise into the warehouses?
d. What level of customer service was needed to stay ahead of competition?
e. How much time is needed for order processing, packing, etc.?
f. Were the added costs for improvements in customer service resultant in an ultimate increment to profits or not?

In his writings on the subject, Clark Sloat cited a simple problem which was easily solved by the use of mathematical programming methods. The problem is shown in Exhibit 3. Notice that the following data is shown in the problem:

Geographic warehouse requirements

Geographic plant manufacturing capacity

Unit production costs by plant

Freight costs per unit from each plant to market

In his simplified problems, Sloat asks two basic questions regarding the problem:

1. How much should each plant produce?
2. Which warehouse should be supplied from which plant?

When the statement of the problem is transcribed in terms of a formal mathematical formula, it can be placed into a preprogrammed computer and the solution evolved in a matter of minutes. The solution to the problem just shown is in Exhibit 4. Sloat, a member of Price Waterhouse & Company, has indicated that use of this type of mathematical technique can produce savings of five to ten percent of the cost of the services, provided that the services have previously been very carefully established. It is his opinion that savings of five to ten percent are fairly representative of achievements.

		Plants				
Warehouse	*Requirements*	1	2	3	4	5
ALTERNATIVE I:						
A	50,000					50,000
B	250,000	30,000	70,000			150,000
C	75,000	75,000				
D	25,000			25,000		
E	30,000			30,000		
F	40,000			40,000		
G	50,000			50,000		
H	200,000				200,000	
I	60,000				60,000	
J	40,000		40,000			
K	20,000			20,000		
L	150,000	145,000		5,000		
M	70,000			70,000		
N	10,000			10,000		
Production		250,000	110,000	250,000	260,000	200,000
Plant capacities		250,000	300,000	250,000	300,000	200,000
Unused plant capacity		0	190,000	0	40,000	0
Unit production cost		$4.00	$3.50	$2.50	$4.00	$3.50
ALTERNATIVE II:						
L		(70,000)		70,000		
M		70,000		(70,000)		
ALTERNATIVE III:						
L		(10,000)		10,000		
N		10,000		(10,000)		

Exhibit 4
Optimum (Minimum Cost) Solution

Avoiding Costly Mistakes

Writing recently in the *Financial Executive*, J. H. Hennessy, Jr. indicated that much faster response times are being achieved both in filling custom orders and in replenishing stocks of real time computer systems and a wide variety of operations research techniques involving advanced inventory and probability theories. As a result, he says that physical distribution has been surprisingly underrated because of the overshadowing preoccupation with computer control for inventory. In those companies which have attempted to remodel the physical distribution systems, some costly mistakes have occurred because the companies did not understand the following:

. . . Did not clearly understand the level of customer service needed in terms of lead time and percent order filling.

. . . Did not realize that the time increments for order processing, picking, and packing quite often make up for large segments of overall required lead time for the distribution of products.

. . . Failed to recognize that small increments of time are involved when shipping distances between source points and customers are extended; nor, on the other hand, how premium shipping modes and faster handling methods can reduce lead times from distant points —approaching the lead time for regular local delivery.

. . . Companies failed to visualize how the variability in demand for regional stocks would increase relative to the increase in number of regional stocking points. This, in turn, requires larger safety allowances and a larger overall inventory carrying penalty for the corporation.

. . . Had misconceptions as to the importance or need for fast delivery on the part of most customers.

. . . Failed to realize that increases in the number of regional stocking points results in increases in the number of back orders within the system.

. . . Did not evaluate the financial tradeoff between improved customer service and added costs.

In order to develop competitive service parameters for the creation of a viable distribution system, Mr. Hennessy created a discussion guide which serves as the basis for developing the distribution model. It is reproduced below. It should be remembered that physical distribution is consuming an increasingly larger part of the revenue dollar.

DISTRIBUTION SYSTEM DISCUSSION GUIDE

(Reprinted by permission from *Financial Executive,* April 1969, J. H. Hennessy.)

Competitive Customer Service

What is competitive service in terms of:

- Delivery cycle time?
- Percent order fill?

What is competitive importance of delivery relative to other competitive influences such as:

- Features or quality of product?
- Price?
- After-market service (i.e., replacement parts for mechanical products)?

What competitive advantages in terms of lower delivered cost of products can be achieved by field inventories:

- Shipping in bulk to major markets?
- Final assembly of products close to major markets?
- Other?

Our Present Customer Service

What is the estimate of present lost orders:

- In dollars?
- As a percent of sales?

What would happen to lost orders if:

- More or fewer items were stocked?
- More or fewer stock locations were employed?
- Higher or lower inventory levels of items presently stocked were carried at present distribution points?

Do lost orders also produce lost customers:

- Does poor delivery merely lose the order on which the delivery is late?
- Does poor delivery not only lose the order in question but cause the customer to go elsewhere on a continuing basis?

Is present customer service competitive:

- Delivery time?
- Line-item fill percentage?
- Order-fill percentage?

- Can we reduce the present inventory investment without other offsetting increases in costs and still meet competition?
- Could we increase the present inventory investment and thereby make a larger percentage return on this investment?

Inventory Profile

Are the items we stock consistent as to physical characteristics such as:

- Size and weight?
- Packaging and shipping characteristics?
- Substance (i.e., metal, fabric, etc.)?
- Storage characteristics (inside, outside, perishable, nonperishable, etc.)?
- Value-density relationships?

If not consistent in what significant classes do they group?
Are items stocked consistent as to markets:

- End use?
- Types of customers (producer, distributor, consumer, etc.)?
- Industrial user classifications?

If not consistent, in what significant classes do they group?
Are items stocked consistent as to demand characteristics:

- Demand consistency?
- Seasonal characteristics?
- Customer service?

Is not consistent, in what significant classes do they group?
What is the number of items in each of the above classes of inventory?
What dollars and percentage of total annual dollar demand do the items in each class represent?

Items Constituting

Class	Top 75% of Sales $	Next 15% of Sales $	Lowest 10% of Sales $	Class Totals
Number of Items				
% of All Items	%	%	%	100%
Sales	$	$	$	$
Average Inventory	$	$	$	$
Sales to Inventory				
% of Class Inventory	%	%	%	100%

Distribution System Profile

How many stocking activities are in existence:

- Factory?
- Regional?
- Territorial?
- Specific products?

How many warehouse facilities are in each type of activity and what is the approximate number of square feet in each:

- Factory?
- Regional?
- Territorial?
- Specific products?

What is the rationale behind the present number and location of stocking points in each distribution plan?

What is the mission of each level or type of distribution activity and how does it relate to the other levels?

What are the total number of items and average inventory investment in each distribution level or type of stock and for the largest and smallest outlets within each level or type?

What is the average inventory turnover in each level of distribution and high-low turnover of outlets at each level and for each product category?

What modes of transportation are in use and under what criteria?

- Common rail carrier?
- Common motor carrier?
- Common air carrier?
- Owned carrier?
- Private carrier?

Do transportation modes and policies differ between master and regional warehouses and territorial depots and/or between stocking points within each of these classes of stocking facilities? If so, how?

Inventory Policies

What products are stored in the plants at which manufactured?

What products are also stored in regional or national master warehouses serving territorial depots and why?

What items are stored in area or local warehouses and why?

What is the criteria for master warehouse stocking?

What is the criteria for regional warehouse stocking?

What is the criteria for local warehouse stocking?

Do the criteria which govern the replenishment of stocks in each of these stocking levels differ and if so how?

Do the criteria differ as to product classes and if so, how?

Are safety stock criteria common for master, regional, and territorial depots, and are they computed on the basis of national, regional, or territorial factors?

Do stocking criteria create pyramiding of stocks between levels?

How are products classified as to movement:

- What are criteria for a fast-moving port?
- What are criteria for other classes—slow-moving, medium, others?

Are criteria predicated on:

- National sales movement?
- Regional or territorial sales movement?
- Combination?

What criteria are used in determining order size and frequency for replenishing inventories in each stocking level:

- Economic lot formula?
- Fixed number of orders divided into annual forecast?
- Fixed order size divided into annual forecast?
- Other?

What criteria are used in establishing order points:

- Fixed order cycle time with provision for a specified percentage variation but uniform demand?
- Fixed order cycle time with provision for demand variations?
- Fixed order cycle time with provision for:
     Variation in cycle time?
     Variation in demand rate?
     Seasonal variations?

How is demand variation measured:

- From forecast sales?
- From historical sales?

If safety stocks are established how is this done:

- Guess of interaction of demand and lead-time factors on stock-out frequency and estimated safety stock required to keep stock-out frequency livable?
- Analysis of demand variations from forecast and application of a factor to the standard deviation to produce a specific frequency of stock-out (i.e., 5% or 1%)?
- Formulation relating demand variation and order quantity to produce:

Minimum recovery period when stock-out occurs?
Minimum pieces on back order between time of stock-out until replenishment takes place?

- Formulation which balances cost of carrying safety stock to lost order cost?

Inventory Practices

What practices are observed with respect to the following:

ORDER PROCESSING

Order Profile:

What are the typical number of line items and shipping and weight characteristics of specific classes of orders, such as:

- Seasonal?
- Product class?
- Customer class?
- Special sales?
- Special handling—i.e., emergency, overseas?
- Other?

What is number of orders received each month in total and for each class?
What are the average, mode, and upper and lower quartiles of line items per order, each month; in total and for each class?
What are the back-order percentages for each of the above classes of orders in terms of number of orders and line items per order?
What differences exist in the uniformity of demand rate for each of the above classes of items?

Order Entry:

Is order entry a centralized function or are orders entered at local warehouses?
What is the order processing sequence and functions and the elapsed time and manhour values for each:

- Mail and registry?
- Edit?
- Credit and special terms?
- Warehouse documents and controls?
- Back-order procedure?

Are items out of stock at one location ordered against stocks in other locations? If so, under what controls?
What is the order time cycle for each class of order such as:

- Large seasonal orders?
- Specific product classes?
- Specific customer type?
- Special handling—i.e., emergency; overseas?
- Other?

Methods and Equipment:

What basic order processing methods are in use:

- Manual?
- Manual—mechanical?
- Unit record (tabulating)?
- Computer:
     Sequential processing?
     Random processing?
- Combination?

What is the number and make of each class of equipment in use in the order entry system?

If rented, what is the annual rental cost?

What is percent utilization of this equipment for the inventory function?

PICKING, PACKING AND SHIPPING

What picking plan is observed—line, zone, or other?

How has the warehouse been laid out?

- Bin trip activity?
- Bin trip density?
- Other?

Where are reserve stocks placed in relation to ready stocks?

How frequently are locations of items in the warehouse established to reflect activity status?

Are individual picking tickets received from order entry?

Are picking tickets presorted into picking sequence to insure optimum picking time?

Are picking tickets for items on back order prescreened to prevent pickers from walking to empty bins?

Are partially filled orders held for complete filling or shipped partial? What factors govern?

Do items requiring emergency handling bypass the normal order entry procedure for expedited picking?

What equipment is used to expedite the order-fill cycle:

- Conveyors?
- Automated pickers?
- Others?

What is the packing procedure:

- Pickers do own checking and packing?
- Separate checkers and/or packers do checking and packing?

What is the average pick-pack time cycle for specific class of orders and products?

What provisions exist for maintaining control over status of orders in process, and for communicating advice to customers on delayed or back-order items?

With respect to specific classes of orders and products what are the manhour requirements per order and per line item for:

- Picking?
- Packing?
- Shipping (loading)?

STOCK STATUS AND REPLENISHMENT

What procedures exist for communicating that a reorder point has been reached at a bin location to the stock control and procurement organizations?

What are the average time requirements for:

- Recognizing that a reorder situation exists?
- Instituting a replenishment order on the vendor or other source?
- Upon receipt of items ordered, communicating the availability of the items received to the inventory control organization?
- Updating of stock status records upon notification of receipt of items by the inventory control organization?

What procedures exist for short-cutting replenishment procedures where items go on back order?

What reports and records exist in connection with stock status, and are these suitable as to format, content, and timeliness?

Are stock status, purchase order, and accounts payable procedures integrated? If not, what advantages are served thereby?

What systems and equipment are used for stock control:

- Manual?
- Manual—mechanical?
- Unit record (tabulating)?
- Computer:

    Sequential processing?
    Random processing?

What are the costs for these activities?

Are the capabilities of the system in terms of stock status reporting appropriately related to the capabilities of the organization to respond to information made available and are they consistent with competitive requirements?

Cost Factors

What is the cost for storing product at the various stocking levels and by types of product:

- Master?
- Regional?
- Territorial?
- Product?

How have, or how should, such costs be developed so that they can be applied to products with different weight-cube-and-value relationships?

What is the cost for handling an order:

- Order processing?
- Picking?
- Packing?
- Shipping?

How are replenishment order sizes determined and what cost factors are applied and how have they been developed?

How have, or how should, such factors be applied to products with different weight-cube-value relationships?

In evaluating different stocking configurations and warehouse operating concepts, how can or should changes in the following factors be reflected by changes in the appropriate cost factors?

- Bin cube utilization?
- Warehouse cube utilization?
- Concentration of stocking closer to packing operations?
- Mechanization and conveyorization?
- Number of items stocked?
- Lead-time periods?
- Stock-out frequency criteria?
- Number and location of stocking points?

How have, or can, freight costs be developed for each mode of transportation to reflect:

- Differences in the weight-cube-value relationships of products?
- Differences in routings?
- Differences in distances shipped?

What changes occur in inventory holding and handling costs with changes in the number of regional or area warehouses, or with changes in their mission, and how are these changes reflected by changes in transportation costs and costs for lost orders?

In a study done approximately twenty years ago, it had been concluded then that distribution costs as defined in the study consumed approximately 60¢ out of every revenue dollar. Although modern valid statistics are not available for the sake of comparison, it is probable that that number has increased certainly to about the 70¢ level. This makes all the more important the acceleration of a program to remodel a physical distribution system based upon the most efficient design which can be produced by the interaction of statistical and probability theory along with plain old commercial horse sense.

MODELS FOR PORTFOLIO MANAGEMENT

Contemporary market analysts are more aware than ever that there are many variables in securities markets and that indeed the variety of these variables has increased in the more recent past. Every technique that is available, including sticking a wet finger to the wind, can and probably should be used for portfolio selection. However, whereas in the past, much portfolio selection was based upon manually and mentally generated subjective evaluations of price earnings ratios, new techniques involving linear programming and quadratic programming have evolved which, at worst, can offer the manager an alternative course of action and an evaluation of the risk that is faced in choosing a portfolio configuration.

Linear Programming

Linear programming is one of the most appropriate techniques for computing the best composition of an investment portfolio. Obviously, the use of such a technique is dependent upon specified investment objectives, constrained by natural and imposed parameters. The two main considerations involved when evaluating any investment are the potential risk involved and the amount of potential return that can be expected within a given time period. Obviously these two factors are mutually independent of each other and vary inversely with each other. In other words, a safe investment carries a lower return than a riskier investment. Using linear programming techniques, it may be possible for a medium risk portfolio, for example, to represent a ninety percent probability of a seven percent return annually. Thus, through the use of this type of logic, a portfolio manager can determine whether it is better to have the ninety percent probability of a seven percent return or a ninety-five percent probability of a six and one-half percent return. Applying the linear programming technique to such problems enables the manager to make this type of decision. The constraints that might be built into a linear programming portfolio problem could involve such typical considerations as:

1. The price earnings ratio cannot exceed sixteen
2. The earnings growth rate must exceed twelve percent
3. Price appreciation must be greater than eighteen percent
4. Yield cannot be less than three percent
5. The range of the yield must be less than one-half percent

Based upon the objectives and the constraints, a linear programming matrix is constructed and as a result of that matrix, a number of solutions may be possible. Without going into specific statistical techniques or complicated examples of sample portfolio problems, it is better said that linear programming is an ideal technique for optimizing portfolio analysis. It does have certain advantages over quadratic programming because it provides greater flexibility and utility.

Quadratic programming deals with constraints, but the constraints are of a secondary nature as compared to the linear programming technique in which these are "first-degree functions." In essence, the linear formulation is better suited for portfolio analysis since any return function may be accommodated and it tends to offer a more realistic approximation of actual conditions.

In addition, many "canned" linear programming computer programs are readily available and are offered for service either by service bureaus or the larger computer concerns. Bond portfolio analysis is a logical extension of securities portfolio analysis with the exception that generally speaking the objective in bond portfolios is to maximize the bond yield, whereas in the securities portfolios analysis, probabilities of appreciation and yields tend to be more important. For those interested in the particular subject, I would commend an article for reading which appeared in the *Financial Executive* in February of 1967 by Alan Bean called "Portfolio Analysis and Stock Selection by Computer."

RISK ANALYSIS MODELS FOR NEW PRODUCTS

An extremely interesting working paper by H. Paul Root at the University of Michigan was recently published dealing with the subject of risk analysis for product innovations. In the context of this working paper, which is an overall document, the computer simulation model developed by Professor Root includes the following components:

The marketing plan

The manufacturing plan
    Capital investment plan
    Manufacturing cost estimates
    Unit variable costs

The financial plan
    Cost estimates for the financial plan
    Other financial estimates

Financial summary information

The computer analysis cost

The importance of this working paper is that the model presented in the paper has been used successfully in real life situations. One corporation which has successfully pioneered in introducing risk analysis models for overall planning has been CPC, International. That company has found that in-house training seminars acquainting personnel with the objectives and techniques employed in the model were the most effective way to achieve the understanding in successful implementation for the model. One of the key factors in their success has been the fact that they made the model more easily accessible to line managers. And the model was explained in depth to selected corporate officers.

Major Types of Plans

The inputs required for each of the major types of plans are as follows:

Marketing Plan
  Unit price
  Promotional expenditures
  Unit sales
  Marketing cost as a percentage of sales

Manufacturing Plan
  Capital investments
  Fixed manufacturing costs
  Capacity limitations
  Variable costs

Financial Plan
  Depreciation
  Other fixed costs
  Costs as a percent of sales
  Working capital requirements
  Tax rate
  Present value discount rate
  Return on investment calculation options
  Terminal year options

The above mass of required input data is specified as required annually or otherwise for products or product types and, most importantly, is expressed in terms of probability of attainment and best estimate.

The computer program was originally written in Fortran IV and has been adopted for a variety of computers ranging up to the new third generation computers currently in use at the University of Michigan. In philosophizing on the results of the sensitivity analysis program, Professor Root made an interesting observation when he said that the implementation of this type of technique has shown that the use of this model can change the behavior of the user in the analysis process. This is an extremely interesting deviant from rationalization that the process often follows the other way around and the tail wags the dog. In any event, the paper is a significant contribution to actual corporate business practice and new product development as it applies to finance.

CONCLUSION

The world of mathematical models for financial planning is growing more sophisticated and is expanding in concept at a frightening rate. One planning model called **PROPHIT** is in existence and uses a modeling concept which will permit the user to prepare alternative solutions to a problem and consequently increase the probability of making a correct business decision. Its virtue is that several possible courses of action can be charted in a very short period of time and, through the use of a terminal, a model can be defined which fits a particular business situation.

Once the model has been defined, a report of projected data and its probable results is available. A typewriter-type terminal is used which is connected to a large service bureau corporation computer center by ordinary telephone service which is installed in the facility of the user. The user is charged for the computer time and the storage which is used. The process is so simple that the data is typewritten at the terminal keyboard; the computer then processes the data and transmits the forecast back to the terminal where it is printed in output form. Not too many years ago this type of procedure would have been considered part of an Alice in Wonderland tradition and would have been much more suitable for a James Bond type of novel than the prosaic environment of the average business executive.

There is no question in my mind that modeling is beneficial and that it is here to stay. What must be carefully evaluated by the potential user is the ability of the user to fully understand and comprehend the limitations of any mathematical formula. Outside of the physical laws of nature, it is the rare event which can be mathematically programmed to behave in a precise manner. No model is the end-all of a decision. It is merely an adjunct to the finger-in-the-wind tradition.